CANDY AISLE
CRAFTS

CANDY AISLE CRAFTS

Create Fun Projects with Supermarket Sweets

JODI LEVINE

PHOTOGRAPHS BY **AMY GROPP FORBES**

FOREWORD BY MARTHA STEWART

POTTER
CRAFT

NEW YORK

For Fred, Sammy, and Lionel, the loves
of my life. And for my mom and dad.
—JODI

For Adam, Oliver, Owen, and Beatrice.
—AMY

Published in the United States by
Potter Craft, an imprint of the
Crown Publishing Group, a division
of Random House LLC, a Penguin
Random House Company, New York.
www.crownpublishing.com
www.pottercraft.com

POTTER CRAFT and colophon are registered trademarks
of Random House LLC.

Library of Congress Cataloging-in-Publication data is
available upon request.

ISBN 978-0-8041-3791-1
eBook ISBN 978-0-8041-3792-8

Printed in China

Book design by Robin Rosenthal
Cover design by Robin Rosenthal
Cover photographs by Amy Gropp Forbes

10 9 8 7 6 5 4 3 2 1

First Edition

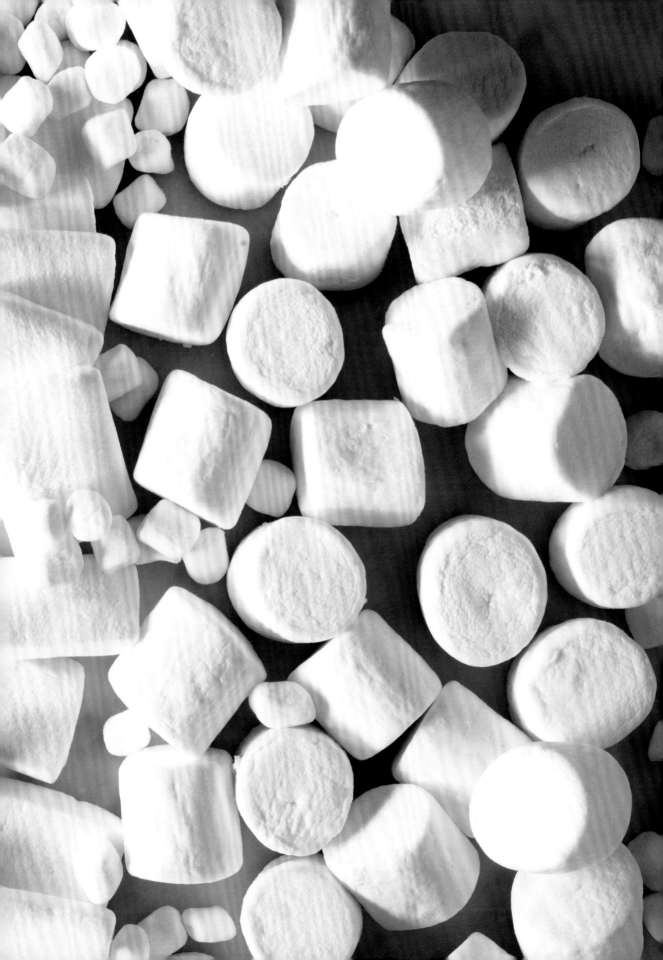

TABLE OF CONTENTS

FOREWORD

JODI LEVINE carried a paper flower bouquet of her own design and fabrication at her wedding in 2000. She wore a dress of taffeta and tulle, which looked as if it had been made with paper coffee filter ruffles and tissue paper flounce (Jodi had also designed a paper dress but was persuaded that it was too perishable in the heat and humidity of August). The table decorations were paper lanterns and crepe-paper blooms—the bridesmaids carried colorful paper fans in pink and pale blue and foil, and the boutonniere was made of small paper blossoms. Our magazine published this charming wedding and called it "A Paper Pastoral." It was a very, very popular story and resonated deeply with so many DIY brides, many of whom emulated the lovely, affordable, but extremely charming ideas at their own weddings.

In the intervening years, Jodi continued her inventive and innovative crafting, and this book is an amusing and inspiring depiction of more of her practical, fun, and inexpensive projects geared to children. Jodi has two active boys who have been sounding boards for her recent craft projects. This book is her gift to us—busy mothers and grandmothers who are always searching for clever ideas, colorful how-tos, and simple, clear instructions using easy-to-find, commonplace materials.

Children and adults alike will love these projects, and afternoons after school and long weekends can now be more creative with Jodi's delightful ideas.

Martha Stewart

INTRODUCTION

AS A KID, I loved combing the aisles of supermarkets for potential supplies for my crafts. Some of my favorite finds were paper plates, doilies, cardboard anything, and candy. Like many kids, I loved candy, but less for eating it than for their colors and shapes and packaging. I thought of it as another craft material possibility. Not that I didn't have a sweet tooth, but baked goodies were more my weakness. I couldn't quite convince my mom to get me these sugary supplies—she didn't buy my story that I wouldn't eat them—and so I got my start in food crafting by making bread dough sculptures out of her scraps, flowers out of cucumber spears, and anything I could using what I found in our kitchen.

My handed-down *Betty Crocker's Cook Book for Boys and Girls* had a formative influence on me. I loved to flip through the pages and see a pear half transformed into a bunny, fudge turtle cookies with pecan arms and legs, and pancakes in the shapes of animals. Food that looked like things! When I was old enough to cook and bake I often turned to this beloved book and made novel desserts, using candy as decorations.

Although I went to art school, I never dreamed I would have a job that allowed me to craft all day long. Luckily enough, I got to do just that working as a craft editor at *Martha Stewart Living*. In my nineteen years there, some of my favorite projects were the crafty food ones. My passion for this kind of work overflowed and I decided that I needed do a book on edible crafts. I love the idea of transforming common food items like marsh-mallows and gumdrops. After mulling over the idea for a few years, I started talking about it with my longtime friend and former colleague, Amy Gropp Forbes. Amy was taking a photography class at the time and I fell in love with the photos she took of her children. Her blog, *Eclectic Mom,* is all about the crafts and projects she does with her family, and our shared interest in these activities prompted me to ask her to partner with me. We had worked together on many kids' stories when she was a food editor at *Martha Stewart Living,* but our friendship deepened when we found out that not only were we pregnant with our firstborns at the same time, but that we even shared the same due date! We both love crafting and cooking with our kids, and we talked and talked for weeks about the idea of doing a book together. Eventually, we agreed that crafts using accessible supermarket materials were really at the heart of what we wanted to focus on, and this book was born.

Some of the prettiest and most craft-friendly edible supermarket materials are candy, but as a mom (like my mom did) I felt conflicted about pushing sugary ideas. Then I thought about the wise Cookie Monster and his realization that there are "anytime" foods and "sometimes" foods. It is exciting to be able to make something magical for "sometimes" occasions like holidays and birthdays with commonplace items from the supermarket. *Candy Aisle Crafts* is full of ideas for parties, holidays, and rainy days that adults and kids can do separately or together. We hope you will enjoy!

MANY OF YOU PROBABLY remember making stained-glass cookies by crushing hard candies and melting them inside a cutout cookie frame. The **stained-glass cookies** in my 1970s *Do a ZOOM Do* craft book were my intro to the endless possibilities of melting hard candies. Later, while attending art school, I had a roommate who was a glassblower, and I became fascinated with **hand-blown millefiori glass** and, eventually, **blown sugar.** I had neither the skills nor equipment to do either. Instead, I started collecting and melting store-bought candy. The projects in this chapter use this technique. Making the colorful candy creations feels like working with glass—and the only equipment needed is an oven!

At holiday time, supermarkets offer a wide variety of candy canes in a whole rainbow of colors, as well as peppermint swirl candies and more. Start collecting these for your candy projects for the whole year. All the brand-name products mentioned in the instructions are things that I found I liked working with, but feel free to experiment with other candies.

While adults should handle the hot work of candy melting, kids can have fun arranging unmelted candies on a cool baking sheet and seeing what results. You'll never quite know how your melted candy will turn out, since happy (and not-so-happy) accidents can happen!

GENERAL CANDY-MELTING TIPS

WARNINGS

The candies can become very hot and you can easily get burned. Before touching hot sugar, always wait at least 30 seconds to 1 minute after taking it out of the oven. Then reshape it by pushing it with the flat front of your fingernail.

Wearing dishwashing gloves while shaping the hot candy can help. Have an oven mitt handy to shield your other hand from the hot baking sheet.

The temperature and timing will vary with different ovens and the size of the candies you are melting.

Always use a kitchen timer and stay near the oven to frequently check the progress of the melting candies.

GENERAL LOLLIPOP-MAKING TIPS

Arrange the candy on one side of the baking sheet to allow room for adding the lollipop stick.

We used wooden skewers, which are available at supermarkets, for sticks. (Cut off the sharp end with kitchen shears; hold the pointy end down into the sink or a garbage bag to catch the pointy end, which tends to go flying when cut.) Alternatively, ready-to-use white paper lollipop sticks are available at craft stores and kitchen supply or baking stores.

Add the stick by pressing it into the bottom of the candy and twisting to coat it with the candy. If this causes wrinkles, you may put it back in the oven for about 30 seconds to 1 minute to smooth it again. This will happen fast, so stay right next to the oven!

All projects call for an oven that's been preheated to 275°F.

If you're cutting candy, cut with heavy-duty kitchen shears or scissors inside a sink or a deep container to catch the candy "shrapnel." Cutting candy while it's still in its wrapper keeps it from flying. Candies can also be crushed by placing them inside a resealable plastic bag and hitting them with a hammer or the back of a metal serving spoon on a cutting board.

Put the candy pieces on a parchment paper-lined baking sheet, arranged as close as possible to your desired design. Leave ⅛" to ¼" between pieces that should be distinct, like a head or tail. They will fuse together during the melting process.

If possible, melt like candies together. Melting times of different brands will vary; for example, Jolly Ranchers melt more quickly than Lifesavers.

If you're making more than one at a time (and especially if they are different sizes and therefore will have different melting times), it is best to keep the various designs on separate pieces of parchment paper so they can be removed separately as needed.

Put them in the oven for 5 to 7 minutes (depending on the size) and stay near the oven. Pull the candy out when it has become smooth and glossy. You do not want to let it melt too much or become bubbly. If the shape has spread too much, let it cool for 1 minute and quickly and carefully push it into the desired shape with the front of the fingernail of your pointer finger.

If the candy is hard to reshape because it is too melty and stringy, let it cool for 30 seconds or more.

When reshaping, make it smaller and tighter, exaggerating shapes since the design will spread a bit more when you put it back in the oven to smooth it out. Return it to the oven and watch it. It may take only 45 seconds or 1 minute for the candy to become smooth.

This craft takes some practice to get used to (how many seconds to wait before reshaping, how to overcompensate in your reshaping when adjusting and remelting).

It's fun to experiment with dropping other colored candies onto already melted candy. I had a lot of happy accidents where I intended to have the candy melt, but had to pull it out of the oven so the rest of it wouldn't overmelt or bubble or burn. Often the barely melted piece made a cool dimensional nose, fin, or the like.

DOT FLOWERS
See how-to, page 16

DOT FLOWERS

(see photo, page 15)

These little dot flower pops, an easy starter project, help you get used to candy melting.

SUPPLIES
parchment paper
1 whole or half Jolly Rancher Bold Fruit Smoothie candy
stick
1 green Jolly Rancher hard candy, cut in half

1. Preheat the oven to 275°F. Line a baking sheet with parchment paper.

2. Place the flower (Fruit Smoothie) candies on the baking sheet.

3. Place in the oven for 3 to 4 minutes. Remove and let cool for 1 minute.

4. Reshape if needed. Add the stick by putting it on the bottom and twisting to coat with candy.

5. Place the green candy pieces on the sides of the stick, slightly overlapping the stick.

6. Return to the oven for 1 to 2 minutes to melt and smooth. Remove from the oven and let cool.

KID-MADE LOLLIPOPS

As I mentioned in the introduction to this chapter, adults should handle the hot work of candy melting, but kids can have fun arranging unmelted candies on a cool baking sheet. The results are always surprising!

SUPPLIES
parchment paper
hard candies (in any color, roughly the same size)
stick

1. Preheat the oven to 275°F. Line a baking sheet with parchment paper.

2. Arrange the candies in a single layer in a circle (or any shape), as shown.

3. Place in the oven and heat for 4 to 6 minutes, until the candy has just fully melted. Remove. Press on a candy stick and twist. Return to the oven for 1 to 2 minutes to smooth, if desired. Remove from the oven and let cool.

VALENTINE POPS

These pops make perfect party favors or school Valentines.

SIMPLE HEART POP

SUPPLIES
parchment paper

2½ cherry Jolly Rancher hard candies or pink Jolly Rancher Bold Fruit Smoothie candies

stick

1. Preheat the oven to 275°F. Line a baking sheet with parchment paper.

2. Arrange the candy on the baking sheet in a V-shape.

3. Place in the oven for about 5 minutes. Remove and let cool for 1 minute.

4. Reshape, if needed, pinching the bottom to make it pointy. Add the stick by putting it on the bottom and twisting to coat with candy.

5. Return it to the oven for 2 to 3 minutes until smooth. Remove from the oven and let it cool on the baking sheet. Press the stick down, if needed. (If needed, let it cool for 1 minute and reshape it.) Return it to the oven for 1 to 2 minutes to smooth. Remove from the oven and let cool.

PEPPERMINT SWIRL VALENTINE POP

Use up leftover peppermint candies from Christmas to make these pops!

SUPPLIES
parchment paper

1 starlight mint candy

1 heart-shaped sprinkle

stick

1. Preheat the oven to 275°F. Line a baking sheet with parchment paper.

2. Put the peppermint candy on the baking sheet.

3. Place the baking sheet in the oven for about 7 minutes. Remove and let cool for 1 minute.

4. Squish on the heart-shaped sprinkle. Shape the candy into a heart, if desired. Put the stick under the candy and press to adhere.

5. Return to the oven for 1 to 2 minutes to allow the candy to adhere to the stick. Remove from the oven and let cool.

ROUND POP WITH INSET HEART

SUPPLIES
parchment paper

2 whole pink Jolly Rancher Bold Fruit Smoothie candies

2 small shards from a cherry red Jolly Rancher hard candy

stick

skewer

1. Preheat the oven to 275°F. Line a baking sheet with parchment paper.

2. Arrange the 2 whole candies on the baking sheet, as shown.

3. Place in the oven for 5 to 6 minutes. Remove and let cool for 1 minute.

4. Reshape and press the candy shards into a V-shape. Add the stick by putting it on the bottom and twisting to coat with candy.

5. Return to the oven for 2 minutes. Remove and let cool for 1 minute. Use the skewer to tug at the heart and shape it.

6. Return it to the oven for 2 to 4 minutes to smooth. Remove from the oven and let cool.

FUNNY FACE LOLLIPOPS

Amy and I talked about including a page of people portrait lollipops. When she suggested that I try making Bert and Ernie–like faces, I was inspired! The "five o'clock shadow" design was a happy accident caused by using two slightly different colors of candy. For the large dimensional noses, I dropped an unmelted candy onto the hot lollipop.

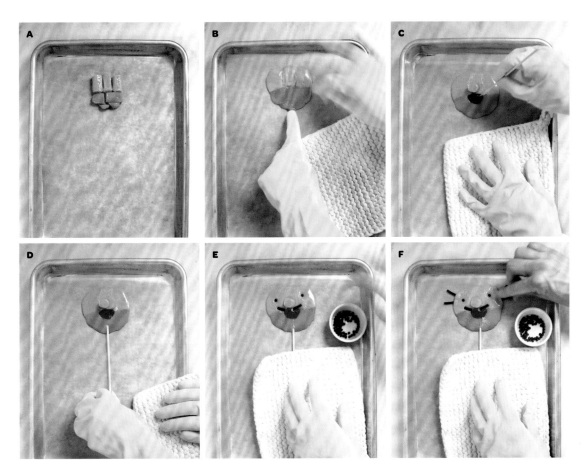

SUPPLIES
parchment paper

2 Jolly Rancher Bold Fruit Smoothie candies (in the desired color for the beard)

scissors

3½ Jolly Rancher Bold Fruit Smoothie candies (in the desired color for the face)

half of 1 cherry Jolly Rancher hard candy

skewer

stick

2 large black nonpareils

4 pieces of black shoestring licorice, cut to ¾"

1. Preheat the oven to 275°F. Line a baking sheet with parchment paper. Cut the beard-colored candies with the scissors to taper the face at the bottom.

2. Arrange the candies on the baking sheet (A). (Reserve the half piece for the nose.) Place in the oven for 5 to 6 minutes.

3. Remove and let cool for 45 seconds to 1 minute.

4. Reshape (B) and press on the red candy for the mouth.

5. Return to the oven for 2 minutes to melt the mouth. Remove and let cool for 1 minute.

6. Use a skewer to tug at the mouth to shape it into a smile and drop on the reserved nose piece (C).

7. Add the stick and twist to cover with candy (D).

8. Press on nonpareils for eyes and licorice for a mustache (E). Tuck licorice hair behind the face (F). Place the baking sheet back in the oven for 2 to 3 minutes to smooth. Remove from the oven and cool on the baking sheet. (Tip: If the nose melts into the face, you can drop a new nose piece on top of the melted one.)

PETAL FLOWERS

Flowers are lots of fun to create, since so many shapes and colors can look floral. For this project, overmelting and undermelting yield interesting and pretty surprises.

RED PETAL FLOWER POP
(1)

SUPPLIES
parchment paper

3 watermelon Jolly Rancher hard candies

3 cherry Jolly Rancher hard candies, cut in half (making 6 half pieces)

stick

1 green apple Jolly Rancher hard candy, cut in half (making 2 half pieces)

1. Preheat the oven to 275°F. Line a baking sheet with parchment paper.

2. Put the 3 watermelon candies on the baking sheet (A).

3. Place in the oven for about 4 minutes. Remove and let cool for 1 minute.

4. Shape the candies into one circle. Press the 6 cherry candy halves around the edge of the large watermelon circle, as shown.

5. Return to the oven for 2 minutes to melt and smooth. Remove and let cool for 1 minute. Add the stick by putting it on the bottom and twisting to coat with candy.

6. Place the 2 green candy halves on either side of the stick, slightly overlapping the stick.

A

B

7. Return to the oven for about 2 more minutes to melt and smooth. Remove from the oven and let cool.

PINK PETAL FLOWER POP
(2)

SUPPLIES
parchment paper

½ cherry Jolly Rancher candy

2½ watermelon Jolly Rancher hard candies, cut in half (for a total of 5 half pieces)

stick

1 green apple Jolly Rancher hard candy, cut in half (making two half pieces)

1. Preheat the oven to 275°F. Line a baking sheet with parchment paper.

2. Put the cherry candy piece on the baking sheet (B).

3. Place in the oven for 1 minute.

4. Remove and arrange the 5 watermelon halves around the cherry candy center, as shown.

5. Return to the oven for 2 minutes. Remove and let cool for 1 minute.

6. Squish the petals down and reshape or separate the petals, if desired. Add the stick by putting it on the bottom and twisting to coat with candy.

7. Place the 2 green candy halves on either side of the stick, slightly overlapping the stick.

8. Return to the oven for about 2½ more minutes to smooth the petals and melt the leaves. Remove from the oven and let cool.

A

B

RED FLOWER WITH WHITE CENTER

(3)

SUPPLIES
parchment paper

1 pineapple (white) Lifesaver

5 cherry Jolly Rancher hard candies

stick

1 green apple Jolly Rancher hard candy, cut in half (making two half pieces)

1. Preheat the oven to 275°F. Line a baking sheet with parchment paper.

2. Put the Lifesaver on the baking sheet (A). Place in the oven for 2 minutes.

3. Remove, cool for 30 seconds, and reshape into a circle, if needed. Arrange the 5 cherry candies around the white center, as shown.

4. Return to the oven for 2 minutes. Remove and let cool for 1 minute. Add the stick by putting it on the bottom and twisting to coat with candy.

5. Place the 2 green candy halves on either side of the stick, slightly overlapping the stick.

6. Return to the oven for about 2½ more minutes to smooth the petals and melt the leaves. Remove from the oven and let cool.

SMALL PINK FLOWER WITH RED CENTER

(4)

The accidental discovery that various candy types require different melting times resulted in an unmelted center for this flower, which I ended up liking. I also like using a Lifesaver leaf for a different shade of green, but feel free to use all Jolly Rancher hard candies, if you prefer. The cinnamon hard candy I used is found in generic hard candy mixes. If you can't find that, half a cherry Jolly Rancher hard candy will work too!

SUPPLIES
parchment paper

2½ watermelon Jolly Rancher hard candies, cut into halves (for a total of 5 half pieces)

1 cinnamon hard candy

stick

½ green Lifesaver

1. Preheat the oven to 275°F. Line a baking sheet with parchment paper.

2. Put the 5 watermelon halves on the baking sheet in a circle (B).

3. Place in the oven for 2 minutes.

4. Remove. Wait 30 seconds, and reshape if needed. Drop the cinnamon candy on the center of the watermelon pieces. Add the stick by putting it on the bottom and twisting to coat with candy.

5. Place the green Lifesaver piece on the side of the stick, slightly overlapping the stick.

6. Return to the oven for 3 to 4 more minutes to smooth and melt leaves (about 2 minutes if you are using all Jolly Ranchers).

7. Remove from the oven and let cool. Squish the Lifesaver leaf to flatten, if needed. The center doesn't have to melt.

CHICK POPS

Chubby chick pops are perfect for a baby shower or an Easter party. Brach's Easter Hunt Eggs make fun additional decorations.

SUPPLIES
parchment paper
2½ Jolly Rancher Bold Fruit Smoothie candies
1 shard of a contrasting color of Jolly Rancher Bold Fruit Smoothie candy
1 black nonpareil
stick

1. Preheat the oven to 275°F. Line a baking sheet with parchment paper.

2. Arrange the candy on the baking sheet, placing the "head" piece ⅛" to ¼" away from the body, as shown.

3. Place in the oven for about 6 minutes. Remove and let cool for 1 minute.

4. Reshape, exaggerating the shape, which will spread when reheated.

5. Add the contrasting-color candy piece as the beak and place the nonpareil as an eye. Add the stick by putting it on the bottom and twisting to coat with candy.

6. Return to the oven for 1 to 2 minutes to smooth. Remove from the oven and let cool.

FISH POPS

Top a cake with these fish pops for an under-the-sea party.

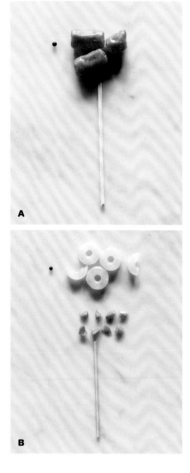

A

B

SOLID ORANGE FISH

SUPPLIES

parchment paper

2½ orange Jolly Ranchers Bold Fruit Smoothie candies

1 black nonpareil

stick

1. Preheat the oven to 275°F. Line a baking sheet with parchment paper.

2. Arrange the candy on the baking sheet with the tail piece ⅛" to ¼" away from the body (A).

3. Place in the oven for about 5 minutes. Remove and let cool for 1 minute.

4. Reshape, exaggerating the shape, especially the mouth and tail, which will spread when reheated.

5. Return to the oven for 1 to 2 minutes to smooth. Remove and let cool for 30 seconds.

6. Add the nonpareil as an eye. Add the stick by putting it on the bottom and twisting to coat with candy. Let cool on the baking sheet.

ORANGE-AND-WHITE-STRIPED FISH POP

SUPPLIES

parchment paper

4 pineapple Lifesavers (3 whole and 1 cut in half)

½ orange Jolly Rancher Bold Fruit Smoothie candy, cut into shards for stripes

toothpick

1 black nonpareil

stick

1. Preheat the oven to 275°F. Line a baking sheet with parchment paper.

2. Arrange the Lifesavers on the baking sheet (B).

3. Place in the oven for about 6 minutes. Remove and let cool for 1 minute.

4. Reshape, exaggerating the shape, which will spread when reheated.

5. Return to the oven for 1 to 2 minutes to smooth. Remove and let cool for 30 seconds.

6. Press the orange candy shards onto the fish in a striped pattern.

7. Return to the oven for 2 minutes.

8. Drag a toothpick through the stripes. Add the nonpareil as an eye. Add the stick by putting it on the bottom and twisting to coat with candy. If needed, return to the oven for 2 minutes to smooth. Let cool on the baking sheet.

TRIANGLE TREE POPS

Making these tree pops gives you a chance to experiment with different textures and patterns. They work well with partially melted whole candies, crushed candies, swirled candies, cut-up candy stripes, and more. You can even add an unmelted candy "tree topper," as on the solid-green tree. Use separate pieces of parchment paper for each tree so you can remove them as they are finished, in case they have different melting times.

SUPPLIES

parchment paper

4 to 5 hard candies for each pop (I used spearmint starlight mints, green apple or blue raspberry Jolly Rancher hard candies, and clear crystal mints)

scissors

stick

1. Preheat the oven to 275°F. Line a baking sheet with small pieces of parchment paper, one for each pop.

2. On one piece of paper, arrange four or five candies to form a rectangle. (For the partially melted starlight mint pop, position four together to make a square, and center another candy at the top.)

3. Place in the oven for 5 to 9 minutes (depending upon how melted you would like your candy). Remove and let cool for 1 minute.

4. Using oven mitts, take the candy, still on the parchment paper, off the baking sheet, and cut it into a triangle or tree shape with scissors, as shown. You can cut through the candy and parchment paper at the same time.

5. Return to the baking sheet on a new piece of parchment, push in or press on a stick, and twist to coat it in candy. If it needs smoothing, return it to the oven for about 2 minutes. Remove from the oven and let cool.

TRIANGLE CAKE DECORATION

These triangular candies could represent trees for a modern Christmas dessert or simply be a graphic cake decoration.

SUPPLIES
parchment paper

4 Jolly Rancher Bold Fruit Smoothie hard candies

scissors

1. Preheat the oven to 275°F. Line a baking sheet with parchment paper.

2. Put the Jolly Ranchers on the parchment in a row to create a tall rectangle. If making more than one at a time, put the candies on individual pieces of parchment, as shown.

3. Place in the oven for 8 to 9 minutes. Remove and let cool for 1 minute.

4. Using oven mitts, take the candy, still on the parchment paper, off the baking sheet, and cut it into a triangle shape (or two smaller triangle shapes) with scissors, cutting through the candy and parchment paper at the same time, as shown.

5. Return to the baking sheet and let cool. Remove the parchment from the triangles.

CIRCUS ANIMALS

These animals would be fun as favors or on a cake.

ELEPHANT

SUPPLIES
parchment paper

2 green apple Jolly Rancher hard candies (1 whole and 1 cut into thirds)

1 green starlight mint candy

2 half-inch-long pieces of candy cane

1 black nonpareil

1. Preheat the oven to 275°F. Line a baking sheet with parchment paper.

2. Arrange the green Jolly Ranchers on the baking sheet, reserving ⅓ piece.

3. Place in the oven for 4½ to 5 minutes. Remove and let cool for 1 minute.

4. Reshape and return to the oven for 2 to 3 minutes to smooth.

5. Remove from the oven and add the starlight mint. Press on the reserved ⅓ piece for the ear. Press on the nonpareil as an eye and press on the candy cane pieces as legs. Let cool.

LION

SUPPLIES
parchment paper

1 orange starlight mint

1¼ orange Jolly Rancher Bold Fruit Smoothie candies

3 black nonpareils

2 half-inch-long pieces of orange candy cane

1. Preheat the oven to 275°F. Line a baking sheet with parchment paper.

2. Put the starlight mint on the baking sheet and place in the oven for 2 minutes.

3. Remove and put the short edge of the whole Jolly Rancher next to it. Heat for 4 to 5 minutes.

4. Remove and let cool for 30 seconds. Gently squish the head to flatten it. Reshape the body. Squish the small Jolly Rancher piece into the center of the starlight mint.

5. Return to the oven and reheat for 2 to 2½ minutes.

6. Remove from the oven. Press the nonpareils onto the face to make the eyes. Press the candy cane pieces onto the body as legs. Let cool.

SEAL

SUPPLIES
parchment paper

2 blue Jolly Rancher hard candies (one whole and one unevenly cut into 1 large and 1 small piece)

2 black nonpareils

1 blue starlight mint candy ball

1. Preheat the oven to 275°F. Line a baking sheet with parchment paper.

2. Arrange the blue Jolly Rancher candies on the baking sheet, as shown.

3. Place in the oven for 4½ to 5 minutes. Remove and let cool for 1 minute.

4. Reshape, exaggerating the shape, which will spread when reheated.

5. Return to the oven for about 2 to 3 minutes to smooth.

6. Remove and add the nonpareils as an eye and a nostril, and press the starlight mint ball onto the nose. Let cool.

BOO AND SPIDER CAKE TOPPER

Forming candy sticks into letters takes a little practice. It's a good idea to have a few extra candy sticks on hand in case one cracks.

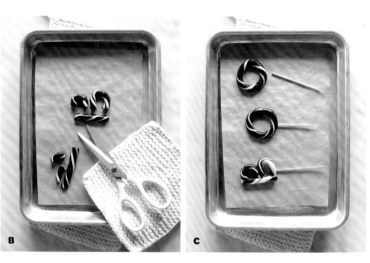

SUPPLIES
parchment paper

4 licorice-flavored candy sticks (plus a few more in case of breakage)

4 wooden skewers

scissors

1 licorice starlight mint candy

8 one-inch-long pieces of black shoestring licorice

1. Preheat the oven to 275°F. Line a baking sheet with parchment paper.

2. To make the *O*s, place two candy sticks on the prepared baking sheet. Heat them in the oven until they look glossy and will bend (stay near the oven!), but before they start to melt and sag, about 3 minutes. Let cool for 30 seconds and gently bend them both into *O* shapes (A).

3. Place skewers under the bottom of the *O*s and return them to the oven for about 2 minutes. Remove from the oven and gently press the candy onto the skewer to secure.

4. To make the *B*, cut off a straight piece of candy as long as the height of your *O*s, about 2¾". Set this to the side of the baking sheet; this will be the straight back line of your letter *B*. Place the remaining scrap and an additional candy stick on the baking sheet. Heat for 3 to 4 minutes until they are glossy but before they start to sag. Remove and let them cool for 30 seconds. Bend each stick into small curved *C*-shaped pieces for the *B*, cutting with the scissors as needed so that they will fit against the straight *B* piece (B). Quickly press the two curved pieces to the straight back reserved

piece and place back in the oven for 2 minutes. Remove. Press back together again if the pieces have shifted apart. Place a skewer underneath the *B* and return to the oven for 2 minutes. Remove from the oven and gently press the candy onto the skewer to secure. Let cool (C).

5. To make the spider, place a licorice starlight mint on the parchment-lined baking sheet and heat in the oven for 4 to 5 minutes or until the candy softens. Remove from the oven, cool for 30 seconds, and carefully place the shoestring licorice "leg" pieces and skewer underneath. Return to the oven for 2 minutes. Remove from the oven, cool for 30 seconds, and gently press the candy onto the skewer and licorice to secure.

HO HO HO CAKE TOPPER

This candy message is an easy cake topper and could also be used on frosted brownies or cupcakes. Place one letter on each brownie or cupcake and spell *HO HO HO* on the tray. Scattering a mix of peppermint candies is a pretty and fast way to decorate a cake stand or platter.

SUPPLIES
parchment paper

3 candy sticks (plus more in case of breakage)

scissors

3 starlight mint candies

1. Preheat the oven to 275°F. Line a baking sheet with parchment paper.

2. Cut the candy sticks into pieces to make three *H*s. Place the pieces on the baking sheet in as close to an H-shape as possible and place in the oven for 3 minutes.

3. Remove from the oven and let cool for about 30 seconds. Gently push the pieces together to adhere. Return to the oven for 1 minute. Remove and gently press pieces together to strengthen the bond. Let cool.

4. To make the *O*s, place the three starlight mints on the cookie sheet and heat in the oven for 4 to 5 minutes, until they have softened and spread slightly. Remove from the oven and let cool.

PEPPERMINT ORNAMENTS

These ornaments are easy to make and would look pretty trimming a mini tree atop a dessert table.

SUPPLIES
parchment paper
starlight mint candies
toothpick
peppermint stick, cut into 1" pieces
candy sticks
baker's twine

1. Preheat the oven to 275°F. Line a baking sheet with parchment paper.

2. For the round ornaments, place starlight mint candies 2" apart on the prepared baking sheet. Heat for 4 to 5 minutes. Remove from the oven and let cool for 1 minute.

3. To make a hole, press the toothpick into the candy and wiggle it around.

4. For the tree ornaments, place two starlight mint candies on the baking sheet right next to each other so their edges are touching. Heat in the oven for 4 to 5 minutes. Remove from the oven and let cool for 1 minute. Press the candies together and shape them into a triangle. Press the candy stick onto the bottom, as shown. Return to the oven for 1 to 2 minutes to adhere. Remove from the oven and add a hole (see step 3).

5. After the ornaments are cool, thread string (such as baker's twine) through the hole and knot.

PEPPERMINT BOWLS

This idea was inspired by millefiori glass bowls. They are an impressive project, but easier to make than you'd think. Some brands of peppermint swirl candies work better than others. Try different types to see which ones work best for you (see Sources, page 107).

SUPPLIES
parchment paper

**heatproof bowl (I used a
6" metal bowl)**

vegetable oil

18 starlight mint candies

scissors

1. Preheat the oven to 275°F.
Line a baking sheet with
parchment paper. Very gener-
ously grease the outside of
the bowl with the oil.

2. Place 1 candy on the
baking sheet.

3. Place in the oven for 2 to
2½ minutes until the candy
starts to look shiny and softens
but doesn't melt or sag.

4. Remove and place six
candies around the heated
candy, touching it (A).

5. Return to the oven and heat
for 4 to 5 minutes. Remove
from the oven as soon as the
candies start to soften. Don't
let them melt.

6. Place eleven more candies
around the circle on the baking
sheet (B). (You can try this
step with nine or ten candies
for a smaller bowl.)

7. Return to the oven for
7 minutes.

8. Remove and let cool for
1 minute. Quickly trim off some
of the parchment paper (C).

With the candy still on the
parchment paper, and using
an oven mitt, flip the candy
onto the greased bowl (D) and
quickly center the middle candy
on the bowl's bottom. Shape
the candy around the bowl,
using the oven mitt to press the
candies into one another (E).
Remove the parchment paper
(F) and gently lift the peppermint bowl off the bowl (it
should slide right off, but if it
sticks, let the candies cool for
another minute or two and
gently pull it off).

9. Place the finished candy
bowls on top of small circles
of parchment paper so they
don't stick to surfaces.

PEPPERMINT BARK DOTS

These dots are inspired both by classic peppermint bark and the fruit- and nut-studded chocolate discs called *mendiants*, a traditional French confection. Each 4-ounce chocolate bar will make about eight to nine 2½" dots. One candy cane (or 2 peppermint candies) will make enough crushed candy topping for each bar.

SUPPLIES

2 candy canes or 4 peppermint candies

resealable bag

hammer

2 four-ounce white chocolate bars

¼ teaspoon vegetable oil (optional)

waxed paper

1. Crush the peppermint candies by placing them in a resealable bag and hitting them with a hammer or the back of a metal spoon.

2. Break the chocolate into somewhat even pieces and put in a stainless steel bowl. Place the bowl on top of a saucepan of simmering water (the bowl should not touch the water). When the chocolate is almost melted, turn off the heat and stir until the chocolate is fully melted. Add up to ¼ teaspoon vegetable oil, if needed, to thin the chocolate.

3. Line a baking sheet with waxed paper. Spoon mounds of chocolate about 1½" in diameter onto the waxed paper, leaving 2" between them. When you have filled the baking sheet, give it a little smack on the counter to smooth and flatten the mounds. Sprinkle the tops with the crushed candies.

4. Refrigerate for at least 30 minutes to harden. Store in an airtight container, separated by layers of waxed paper, in the refrigerator.

CANDY CANE HEART PENDANT

Like the Peppermint Swirl Valentine Pops (page 18), these are an excellent way to use leftover Christmas candy!

SUPPLIES
parchment paper
scissors
2 hooked candy canes
string

1. Preheat the oven to 275°F. Line a baking sheet with parchment paper.

2. Use scissors to cut off the C-shaped hooked ends of the candy canes at an angle so the cut ends of each will fit together to form a heart. (If needed, use scissors to gently cut off a tiny bit at a time, shaving away the ends to smooth the angles.)

3. Arrange the two candy pieces on the baking sheet to form a heart shape.

4. Place in the oven for about 3 minutes until they start to look glossy but don't melt or sag. Remove and nudge the pieces together. If needed, return the candy to the oven for another 30 seconds to 1 minute to adhere.

5. Let cool. Hang the heart from a string to make a necklace or an ornament.

IF YOU ARE LOOKING to make an edible craft—perhaps to top a cake or cupcake or for a party activity—gummy candy, which comes in every shape, color, and size, is the perfect material. Once cut, the sticky interior of a gummy candy allows pieces to be easily stuck together. The soft candy we used in this chapter includes **classic gumdrops and spice drops, gummy letters and rings, chewing gum, colored licorice, shoestring licorice, sour belts, and more,** as well as some old nongummy friends like jelly beans and Necco Wafers. I've found that the candy aisle at many drugstores offers an amazing variety at reasonable prices. Gumdrops—those familiar fat sugarcoated candies—and spice drops, their smaller cousins, are essential crafting materials for many of the creatures here. **Sour belt candy,** a flat sugarcoated gummy "tape," comes in green, making it perfect for creating flower leaves, and red, which I use for mouths and tongues. I've found it at many corner candy and newspaper shops in my neighborhood, but it's also available at specialty candy stores or online.

Familiarize yourself with the wide range of shapes and sizes of sprinkles and tiny candies that are available—like round nonpareils or jumbo nonpareils; long, skinny sprinkles (aka "jimmies"; red ones are perfect for making creature mouths); and mini M&M's (see Sources, page 107). Gather a stash of candies that will be your toolkit of supplies for edible crafts. You'll be ready for every birthday party and holiday!

GENERAL GUMMY CANDY CRAFTING TIPS

Gumdrops and spice drops look very similar, but the gumdrop is larger than the spice drop.

In these directions, the "top" of the gumdrop or spice drop is the rounded part and the "bottom" is the flat part.

I found that if you pluck the tiny round black sprinkles off Haribo Raspberry candies, they make great eyes!

GUMMY LETTER NECKLACES

Personalized candy necklaces are cute party favors and—better yet—a fun party activity. Set out string, plastic needles (don't worry, they aren't sharp!), and bowls of candy, and let the kids make these themselves.

Prepiercing the holes is a must for smaller kids. Firm gummies, like letters, fish, and bears, are less sticky than soft gummy candies, such as gumdrops, and leave less goo on the string, making them easier to slide onto the necklace. Snip up some colored licorice, such as Twizzlers Rainbow Licorice Twists, which make instant beads that require no piercing.

SUPPLIES
scissors

baker's twine

gummy letters and assorted candies

Twizzlers Rainbow Licorice Twists, cut into 1" to 1½" "beads"

heavy sewing needle, such as a tapestry or darning needle

plastic needle

1. Cut the twine into lengths long enough that, once tied, the necklaces will easily fit over a child's head.

2. Put the candy into separate bowls. Use the heavy sewing needle to prepierce holes where needed.

3. Thread the plastic needle with the twine.

4. Thread the candies onto the twine in your desired design.

5. Tie the ends of the twine together to finish the necklace.

I LOVE YOU CAKE TOPPER

Gummy letter toppers are perfect for those who are uncomfortable with a piping bag but want to personalize a cake. Spell out any short message, like *I LOVE YOU*, or someone's name.

SUPPLIES
gummy letters, such as Haribo Alphabet Letters

12" wooden skewers (or shorter, like 10", if you're only making a one- or two-line message)

scissors (optional)

1. Select the necessary letters from the bag of candy. Poke the pointy end of a skewer into the bottom of each letter.

2. Use scissors to cut some skewers shorter, if desired, to stack words, as shown. Poke the skewers into the top of a cake.

3. Be sure to remove skewers before cutting and serving the cake.

NECCO GUMDROP FLOWERS

Remember Necco Wafers? These retro flat, round candies make perfect petals on a gumdrop flower. Use the sugary blooms to decorate the edge of a glass or the top of a cupcake.

SUPPLIES
4 Necco Wafers

1 gumdrop

butter or paring knife (optional)

1. Push the edge of a wafer into the gumdrop, about halfway up the side of the gumdrop. Repeat with the remaining wafers.

2. To hang off the edge of a glass, use the knife to cut a slit that's about ¾" wide just under one of the wafers and slide the slit onto the glass rim.

NECCO GUMDROP BEES

These little bees like to land on glasses of lemonade, and also on cupcakes. They are ideal for a flower- or bug-themed kids' party. If you want to make a butterfly instead of a bee, break two wafers in half and pierce into a spice drop, as shown, opposite.

SUPPLIES
1 white Necco Wafer

scissors

1 black gumdrop (or 1 spice drop for a mini bee)

1 yellow gumdrop (or 1 spice drop for a mini bee)

butter or paring knife (optional)

1. Break the Necco Wafer in half. These will be the wings.

2. Cut off the top third of the black gumdrop. This will be the head. Cut off the bottom of the gumdrop to expose the stickiness. This will make the black stripe.

3. Cut off the top third of the yellow gumdrop and discard. Cut the remaining piece in half horizontally, as shown.

4. Stack the candy pieces as shown, sticky sides to sticky sides, creating the bee's stripes.

5. Push the Necco Wafer wings into the sides of the bee.

6. To hang it off the edge of a glass, use the knife to cut a slit that's about ¾" wide, and slide the slit onto the glass rim.

GUMDROP BOAT CUPCAKE TOPPER

Place this sweet little boat onto a cupcake frosted with light blue icing that's been swept into peaks, like choppy water. If you can't find Fruit Stripe gum, sour belt candy is another great option for the sail, as shown, opposite.

SUPPLIES
scissors

1 piece of Fruit Stripe gum

1 toothpick

1 gumdrop

1 blue frosted cupcake

1 blue cupcake paper (optional)

1 eight-inch-long piece of baker's twine (optional)

1 gummy ring (optional)

1. Cut the gum into a sail or flag shape. Poke a toothpick into the bottom left side.

2. Poke the other end of the toothpick into the bottom of a gumdrop, which is the boat.

3. Optional: Use scissors to cut wave shapes into the top of the blue cupcake paper and put it under the cupcake. Tie the twine around the gummy ring and poke the other end into the frosting.

4. Put the completed boat onto the frosted top of the cupcake.

FROG ON LILY PADS

Making this plump little frog is another fun activity for kids. Show them the animals on the Gummy Animal Menorah (page 62), and they will see more of the many ways to transform gummy candy into little creatures. Once again, these make for a cute cupcake topper!

If you can't find Fruit Imperials to use for the eyes, you can roll tiny pieces of white gumdrop, or use white sugar pearls or candy eyeballs, like those made by Wilton and found at most big box stores (see Sources, page 107).

SUPPLIES
scissors

2 green gumdrops

1 red sour belt candy

toothpick

2 white Fruit Imperials

2 black nonpareils or a black food coloring marker (for eyes)

1 red and 1 green gumdrop (optional)

green Necco Wafers (optional)

1. For the feet, cut two small pieces off one of the green gumdrops and set aside.

2. Cut the sour belt into a long tongue shape.

3. Use the scissors to cut a slit in the side of the second green gumdrop. Squeeze the gumdrop slightly to open the slit and insert the tongue.

4. With the toothpick, scrape away some sugar coating to expose stickiness on two spots where you'll put the eyes. Press on the white Fruit Imperial for eyes. Use the toothpick to scrape a tiny bit of gumdrop goo from the green scrap onto the Fruit Imperials and adhere the black nonpareils to add pupils (or add black dots with a food coloring marker).

5. Cut away some of the sugary coating on the body to make two sticky spots for the feet to go. Cut the back off the two feet pieces and adhere them to the sticky spots.

6. To make the water lily (optional): Cut off the flat bottom of a green gumdrop and leave it sticky side up. This will be the lily pad. Snip seven tiny petals off a red gumdrop. Arrange them, as shown, on the sticky top of the lily pad. Scatter some green Necco Wafers around for extra lily pads.

BALL GOWN LADIES CUPCAKE TOPPERS

Here are some fancy lady cupcakes to dress up a tea party or a ballet-themed party. Switch out the spice drop and M&M colors to change the ladies' hair and skin color. I used cupcake papers dip-dyed with food coloring for skirts, but any solid or patterned cupcake paper would work. There are so many fun prints available now online and in party stores—and, yes, even at supermarkets!

SUPPLIES
scissors
1 white spice drop
1 black spice drop
1 brown mini M&M
toothpick
2 black nonpareils
1 red sprinkle
1 red gumdrop
2 cupcake papers,
stacked
1 white frosted
cupcake

1. To make the head, cut off a piece of the white spice drop diagonally from top to bottom to make a spot for the hair to be placed. Cut off the same shape from the black spice drop. Use the smaller black cut piece as hair and adhere to the cut spot on the larger white piece, as shown. Cut a tiny piece off the top of the black "hair" and press on the brown M&M "bun."

2. To make the eyes and mouth, use the toothpick to poke two holes for eyes and scrape a line for the mouth. With the now-sticky toothpick, pick up the nonpareils and push them into the holes. Press the red sprinkle on the mouth line.

3. To make the body, cut off the top of the red gumdrop and press the head onto that sticky spot.

4. Cut off a thin slice of the bottom of the gumdrop body and adhere it to the overturned cupcake papers "skirt." Place the lady on top of the cupcake.

LION CUPCAKE TOPPER

Roar! These plump little lions are a good treat for a safari- or circus-themed party (along with the clowns on page 61). I love cake and cupcake toppers that require just a few items and no fancy piping skills. Get the kids to help prep these while you bake the cupcakes!

SUPPLIES
toothpick

1 yellow gumdrop

3 black nonpareils

scissors

black shoestring licorice or Haribo Black Licorice Wheels

4 yellow cupcake papers (if the papers have white insides, turn the papers inside out so the yellow side is facing up)

1 yellow frosted cupcake

1. To make the eyes and nose, use the toothpick to poke two holes for eyes and one for the nose into the top of the gumdrop. With the now-sticky toothpick, pick up the nonpareils and push them into the holes.

2. Use the toothpick to scrape away some of the sugar on the yellow gumdrop to expose stickiness on the head where the whiskers will be placed.

3. To make the whiskers, cut off two ½" pieces of the licorice, and cut each piece in half lengthwise about halfway. Spread open the split pieces. Press the whiskers into the face.

4. Make a stack of three cupcake papers (using more than one cupcake paper prevents a big grease stain from bleeding through the cupcake paper once you press it onto the frosting). Put the face inside the papers.

5. To make the tail, cut a tail shape from the remaining cupcake paper, as shown.

6. To make the legs, cut two 1"-long pieces of licorice.

7. Place the head on the cupcake off to one side. Gently push the tail into the frosting on the other side. Gently push the two legs into the frosting below.

CLOWN CUPCAKE TOPPER

Happy clown cupcakes are perfect (along with the lions on page 59) for a circus-themed party.

SUPPLIES
scissors

1 striped (or solid) cupcake paper

1 orange (or any light-colored) gumdrop

1 blue sour belt candy

toothpick

2 black nonpareils

red shoestring licorice or Twizzlers Pull 'n' Peel

3 red mini M&M's

1 white frosted cupcake

1. To make the collar, cut the cupcake paper in half. Turn it inside out, if necessary, to reveal the pattern.

2. To make the face, cut the rounded top off the gumdrop. Turn it over so the sticky side is down and press it onto the collar, as shown.

3. To make the hat, cut a slit into the top of the head. Cut a triangular piece of the sour belt candy, and push the hat into the slit.

4. To make the eyes, use the toothpick to poke two holes into the gumdrop. With the now-sticky toothpick, pick up the nonpareils, and push them into the holes.

5. To make the mouth and nose, use the toothpick to scrape away some of the sugar to expose stickiness on the head where the mouth and nose will be placed. Press on a ⅝" piece of licorice for the mouth and an M&M for the nose.

6. Place the head at the top of the cupcake. Drop the two M&M buttons below in a row.

7. For the arms and legs, cut four 1" pieces of licorice. Gently push the arms and legs into the sides and bottom of the frosting, as shown.

GUMMY ANIMAL MENORAH

Have a menorah-making party! Kids can make these animals, or any gumdrop creation they dream up, and group them together for a novel Hanukkah menorah. All these animals would also make great individual cupcake candleholder toppers for a birthday party. Prepierce a hole for a birthday candle if you're using the creatures for a menorah or candleholder.

FOX

SUPPLIES
scissors
3 orange gumdrops
toothpick
2 black nonpareils
1 brown mini M&M

1. To make the head, cut a piece off the side of one gumdrop, cutting vertically with the rounded part at the top. Snip off a tiny bit of the rounded top to make a sticky spot for the nose. Press the mini M&M onto the sticky spot.

2. Use the toothpick to poke two holes in the top of the gumdrop for the eyes. With the now-sticky toothpick, pick up the nonpareils, and push them into the holes.

3. To make the ears and tail, take the second orange gumdrop and cut two triangular pieces for ears and one piece off the side for the tail. Use the toothpick to scrape away some of the sugar from the gumdrop to expose the stickiness where the ears will be placed. Press on the ears.

4. To make the body, take the third orange gumdrop and cut off the rounded top and one side. Press on the head and tail.

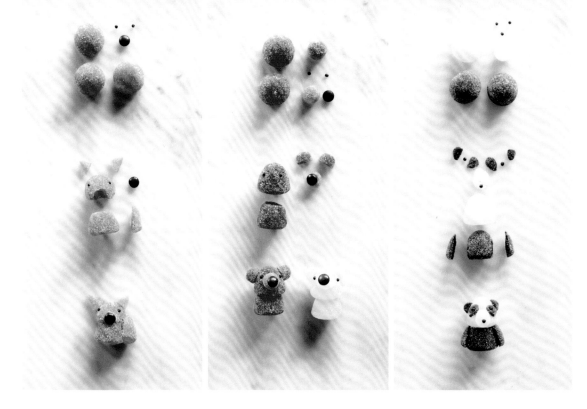

RED (OR YELLOW) BEAR

SUPPLIES
scissors
2 red (or yellow) gumdrops
1 red (or yellow) spice drop
toothpick
2 nonpareils
1 orange (or white) spice drop
1 brown mini M&M

1. Cut a tiny piece off the top of one of the red gumdrops to expose the stickiness. This is the body.

2. Cut the red (or yellow) spice drop in half lengthwise, and again widthwise. The two top rounded quarters will be the ears

3. On the remaining red (or yellow) gumdrop, using the toothpick, poke two holes for eyes. With the now-sticky toothpick, pick up the non-pareils, and push them into the holes. Scrape away two spots for the ears and press them on.

4. To make the snout, cut the rounded tip off the orange (or white) spice drop, and push the M&M onto the end of it. Cut off the back of the spice drop. Scrape off some sugar to make a sticky spot for the snout, and press it on the face.

5. Press the head onto the sticky cut spot on the body gumdrop.

PANDA

SUPPLIES
scissors
2 black gumdrops
1 white spice drop
toothpick
3 black nonpareils
1 white gumdrop

1. To make the arms, cut off two thin slices from the sides of one of the black gumdrops. From the remaining piece of gumdrop, cut four small pieces: two for the eye spots and two for the ears.

2. To make the snout, cut off the bottom of the white spice drop at an angle.

3. Use the toothpick to poke two holes in the eye spots for eyes. With the now-sticky toothpick, pick up the nonpareils, and push them into the holes. Poke a hole on the snout and push the last nonpareil in as a nose.

4. Use the toothpick to scrape off some sugar from the white gumdrop to expose the sticki-ness where the ears, eyes, and snout will go. Press on the eyes, ears, and snout.

5. Cut a tiny piece off the top and sides of the remaining black gumdrop. Press the arms and the head to the sticky cut parts.

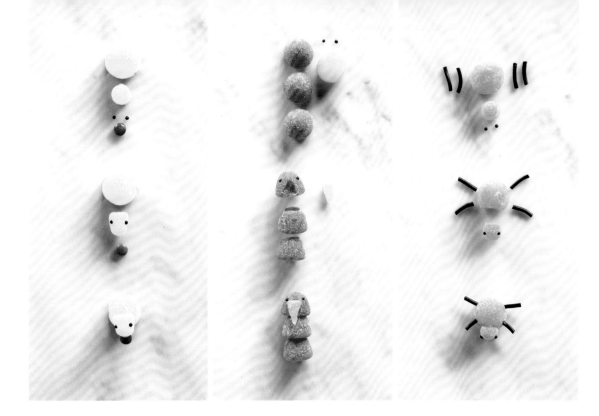

DUCK

SUPPLIES
scissors
1 yellow gumdrop
toothpick
1 yellow spice drop
2 black nonpareils
1 orange mini M&M

1. Cut a small angled piece off the side of the top of the gumdrop. This is where the head will be attached.

2. Use the toothpick to poke two holes in the side of the spice drop for eyes. With the now-sticky toothpick, pick up the nonpareils and push them into the holes.

3. Cut a piece off the bottom edge of the spice drop head and adhere it to the gumdrop body.

4. To make the beak, cut a slit in the front of the head and push in the mini M&M.

ORANGE BIRD

SUPPLIES
scissors
3 orange gumdrops
1 yellow gumdrop
toothpick
2 black nonpareils

1. Cut the tops off two of the orange gumdrops. Stack them together.

2. To make the beak, cut a triangular piece off the yellow gumdrop.

3. Cut a tiny piece off the side of the third orange gumdrop and press on the yellow beak. This will be the head.

4. Use the toothpick to poke two holes for eyes. With the now-sticky toothpick, pick up the nonpareils, and push them into the holes.

5. Press the head onto the body (the top of the two stacked orange gumdrops).

TURTLE

SUPPLIES
scissors
1 green gumdrop
toothpick
1 green spice drop
2 black nonpareils
4 pieces black shoestring licorice (such as Haribo Black Licorice Wheels), each about ¾" long

1. Cut a tiny piece off the side of the gumdrop.

2. Use the toothpick to poke holes in the side of the spice drop for eyes. With the toothpick, pick up the nonpareils and push them into the holes.

3. Use the toothpick to poke two holes in each side of the gumdrop for the arms and legs. Dig around to enlarge the hole so that the licorice will fit. Push the licorice into each hole.

4. Cut a bit off the back of the head, and press it onto the cut sticky front of the body.

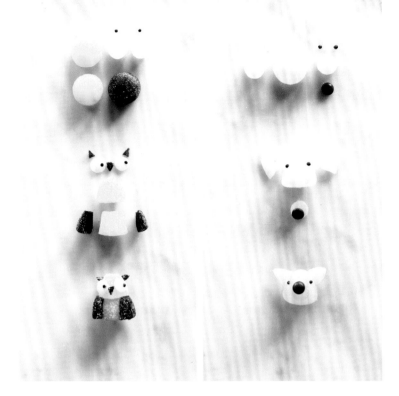

OWL

SUPPLIES
scissors
2 yellow gumdrops
1 black gumdrop
2 white spice drops
toothpick
2 black nonpareils

1. To make the body, cut off the sides and top of one yellow gumdrop.

2. To make the wings, cut off the sides of the black gumdrop. Adhere these to the cut sides of the body. Save the scrap gumdrop.

3. To make the ears and beak, using the black gumdrop scrap, cut two tiny triangles for the ears and one slightly larger triangle for the beak.

4. To make the eyes, cut off the tops of the two white spice drops. Use the toothpick to poke two holes for pupils. With the now-sticky toothpick, pick up the nonpareils, and push them into the holes.

5. To make the head, use the toothpick to scrape away some of the sugar to expose stickiness on the remaining yellow gumdrop where the eyes, ears, and beak will be placed. Press on the eyes, ears, and beak. Press the head onto the body.

POLAR BEAR HEAD

SUPPLIES
scissors
2 white spice drops
toothpick
1 white gumdrop
2 black nonpareils
1 brown mini M&M

1. To make the ears, cut two triangular pieces off the side of one of the spice drops.

2. To make the eyes, use the toothpick to poke two holes in the white gumdrop. With the now-sticky toothpick, pick up the nonpareils and push them into the holes.

3. To make the snout, snip a small piece off the rounded tip of the remaining spice drop, and push on the M&M. Cut the back off the snout.

4. Use the toothpick to scrape away some of the sugar on the gumdrop to expose stickiness where the ears will be placed. Press on the ears.

I'VE CREATED COUNTLESS THINGS out of marshmallows. In my job as a craft editor for *Martha Stewart Living* magazine I made marshmallow ghosts to top a cake, marshmallow skulls, and more. My kids and I built marshmallow "molecules" by poking toothpicks into them. I made marshmallow sculptures and we even had a marshmallow blaster birthday party! When Amy and I started work on this book, I feared I had tapped out all the **marshmallow-crafting** possibilities. But after playing with them a bit more I became convinced that the possibilities were endless!

Marshmallows are the ultimate crafting material. Once cut, they stick to themselves beautifully—no glue or toothpick skewering required. And with the discovery of jumbo marshmallows—plus flat, pink (strawberry), chocolate, peppermint, and novelty-shaped marshmallows—the project ideas are seemingly innumerable. When I couldn't locate jumbo or flavored marshmallows at my supermarket, I found them at big box stores. **Every time I went back to buy more, I spotted new types:** heart-shaped, stars, pumpkins, peppermint swirls, Christmas trees, and more. For the crafts in this chapter, we stuck with the ones that are available year-round. One kind, flat marshmallows (Kraft's Jet-Puffed StackerMallows), are meant for s'more-making but are perfect for pushing a cookie cutter through (see page 82). Once you and your kids start playing with them, I guarantee you'll **come up with lots of fun ideas!**

COW ON A MUG

This cow is "grazing" on a cup of chocolate milk!

SUPPLIES
scissors

1 regular marshmallow

1 chocolate-flavored marshmallow (I used Kraft Jet-Puffed Chocolate Royale Marshmallows)

toothpick

4 black nonpareils or 4 sprinkles from a Haribo Raspberry candy

1 black Haribo Raspberry candy

1 jumbo marshmallow

1. To make the head, cut the regular marshmallow in half horizontally and turn it on its side. The flat uncut bottom will be the face. Cut the chocolate marshmallow in half horizontally, and press the cut sticky side of one half to the face to make the snout. Use the toothpick to poke two holes for eyes and two for nostrils. With the toothpick, pick up the nonpareils and push them into the holes. Cut a thin sliver off the top of the head and adhere the raspberry candy "hat."

2. To make the body, cut a slit along the long side of the jumbo marshmallow. Push the slit onto the rim of a mug. Trim a bit off one edge of the jumbo marshmallow and a bit off the bottom of the head to expose their stickiness and press together.

PIGGY CUPCAKES

These cupcakes are perfect for a barnyard-, pink-, or piggy-themed party (really, my friend's niece had a piggy party!). Make your favorite cupcakes and ice them with vanilla frosting tinted pink with a few drops of red food coloring.

SUPPLIES
scissors

1 Kraft Jet-Puffed Strawberry Marshmallow

toothpick

4 black jumbo nonpareils

1 pink frosted cupcake

1. To make the nose, cut a marshmallow in half horizontally, reserving the scrap. Use the toothpick to poke two nostril holes into the uncut flat side of the marshmallow. With the now-sticky toothpick, pick up a black sugar pearl and push it into a hole. Repeat for the other nostril. Press the nose onto the center of the cupcake. Push the remaining two black sugar pearls into the cupcake as eyes.

2. To make the ears, cut two triangular pieces from the reserved marshmallow scrap (as shown on page 70 for the bird's head) and press them onto the frosted edge of the cupcake.

BIRDS

Experiment with head angles to give your birds different personalities!

SUPPLIES
scissors
2 to 3 regular marshmallows
toothpick
2 black nonpareils
pretzel sticks (optional)
gumdrops (optional)
large shredded wheat (optional)

1. To make the head and neck, cut one marshmallow at an angle, as shown, reserving the scrap. Use the toothpick to poke two holes for eyes. With the now-sticky toothpick, pick up the nonpareils and push them into the holes.

2. Take the reserved marshmallow scrap and trim off a small sticky piece for the neck.

3. If you're making wings, cut at an angle two larger pieces of the second marshmallow.

4. To make the torso, the remaining marshmallow can be used horizontally or vertically, as shown. Trim off three spots for the head and two wings (if you're making wings). Press the neck, head, and wings onto their spots.

5. If you're making the standing bird, poke two holes for the pretzel stick legs and push them in. Poke two holes in one or two gumdrop "rocks" and push the bottom of the pretzel legs

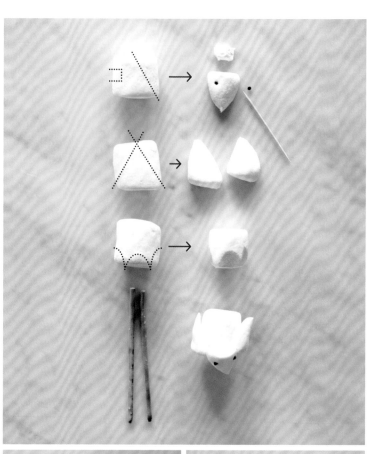

so the bird is standing up (two holes in one "rock" for a standing bird and one hole each in two "rocks" for a walking bird).

6. For a pretzel nest, lay down 10 to 15 pretzel sticks, overlapping them in a circular pattern with the ends sticking

out. Gently place a seated bird on top.

7. For a shredded wheat nest, break off the bottom of one end of the piece of shredded wheat and place a seated bird in the hollow inside.

MONSTER S'MORES

These scary s'mores, a perfect Halloween treat or activity, are made in the broiler. They turn golden very quickly, in as fast as 45 seconds, and can burn before you know it, so stay right next to the oven with your oven mitt on!

SUPPLIES
parchment paper

assorted flat cookies (such as honey or chocolate graham crackers, Nabisco Famous Chocolate Wafers, and tea biscuits)

thin flat chocolate bars (such as Hershey's)

scissors

regular and mini marshmallows

toothpick

regular and mini chocolate chips

1. Preheat the broiler.

2. Line a baking sheet with parchment paper. Arrange the cookies on the baking sheet and put a piece of the chocolate bar on top of each one.

3. To make the eyes, cut mini or regular marshmallows in half horizontally. Arrange the halves on top of the chocolate, sticky side down. Poke holes in the marshmallows with the toothpick, and dig around to enlarge the holes. Push a mini or regular chocolate chip into each hole, pointy side down.

4. To make the teeth, cut angled pieces off the remaining mini or regular marshmallows and press the cut sides into the chocolate.

5. Put the baking sheet in the oven and watch carefully. Remove as soon as the s'mores turn golden, about 45 seconds. Let them cool until they're just warm before handling or eating.

MAMA POLAR BEAR

The mama polar bear and her baby are watching over a pale blue–frosted cake full of arctic friends. For a baby bear, use a regular marshmallow for the head and torso, and cut another into quarters for the legs.

SUPPLIES
scissors

2 jumbo marshmallows (or 2 regular ones, for baby)

toothpick

2 black nonpareils

1 brown mini M&M

1 mini marshmallow

2 regular marshmallows

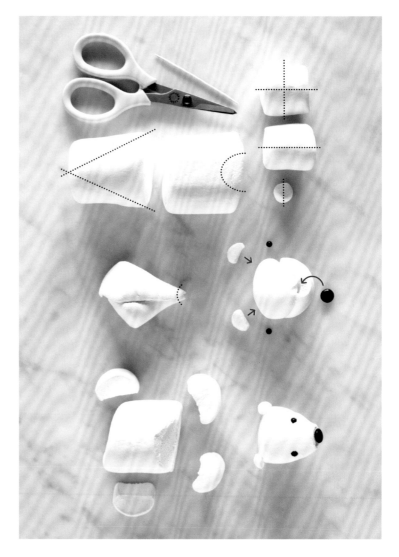

1. To make the head, cut off two triangular pieces from one of the jumbo marshmallows, as shown, and stick the cut sides together. Use the toothpick to poke two holes for eyes. With the now-sticky toothpick, pick up the nonpareils and push them into the holes.

2. To make the nose, cut off the pointiest tip of the head, and press on the mini M&M.

3. To make the ears, cut the mini marshmallow in half horizontally. Cut one of those pieces in half vertically. Press the flat, sticky edges to the head.

4. To make the torso, cut an angled spot off the second jumbo marshmallow to expose stickiness where the head will go. Cut a flat sliver off the bottom of the head to expose stickiness, and adhere it to the torso.

5. To make the legs, cut two regular marshmallows in half vertically. Press two of the pieces onto the torso to create the front legs. Cut one of the remaining halves in half horizontally. These will be the hind legs. (Save the remaining half marshmallow to make another bear.) Press onto the rear bottom of the torso.

PENGUINS

Mama and baby penguin cuddle next to a pile of rock candy ice.
Note that for the penguin baby, you use only one black gumdrop for the
body and a black Haribo Raspberry for the head. Add the beak by
scraping away some raspberry sprinkles and skip the nonpareil eyes.

SUPPLIES
scissors

1 regular marshmallow

2 black gumdrops

toothpick

2 black nonpareils

1 orange gumdrop

1. To make the mama penguin torso, cut a sliver off the flat top of the marshmallow where the head will go. Cut two angled sides where the wings will be adhered.

2. To make the wings, cut two slim pieces off the side of a black gumdrop. Press the pieces onto the cut sides of the marshmallow.

3. To make the head, on the side of the remaining black gumdrop, use the toothpick to poke two holes for eyes. With the now-sticky toothpick, pick up the nonpareils and push them into the holes.

4. Cut an angled piece off the side of the orange gumdrop for the beak. Roll it between your fingers to make it pointy. Cut a sliver off the back of the beak so that it is sticky. Use the toothpick to scrape away the sugary coating on the black gumdrop head to expose some stickiness, and press on the beak. Press the head onto the body.

BUNNIES

Quick to make, these sweet bunnies are perfect cupcake toppers for Easter or a baby shower.

SUPPLIES
scissors

2 regular marshmallows

toothpick

2 black nonpareils

1 large pink nonpareil

cupcake paper filled with colored sanding sugar (optional)

1. To make the head, cut off a fat piece along the cylinder edge of the flat bottom of one of the marshmallows, as shown.

2. To make the ears, along the other edge of the marshmallow, cut two long skinny pieces and stick them to the sides of the head.

3. To make the face, use the toothpick to poke two holes for eyes and one for the nose. With the now-sticky toothpick, pick up the black nonpareils and push them into the holes for the eyes. Push the pink nonpareil into the hole for the nose.

4. To make the body, cut away a scoop on the edge of the remaining marshmallow, as shown. Press the head onto the marshmallow. (Cut away more of the body marshmallow, if needed, to adhere the head.)

5. Nestle the bunnies in cupcake papers filled with colored sanding sugar (as shown) or on top of cupcakes.

SEAL

This seal is sliding around on some ice (aluminum foil) surrounded by drifts of snow (sugar). He is made with a technique similar to the bunnies, except without ears and with flippers. See page 75 for a cake featuring the seal with some of his arctic friends!

SUPPLIES
scissors
3 regular marshmallows
toothpick
3 black nonpareils
aluminum foil (optional)
sugar (optional)

1. To make the head, cut off a fat piece along the cylinder edge of the flat bottom of one of the marshmallows, as shown in the Bunnies how-to (opposite).

2. To make the face, use the toothpick to poke two holes for eyes and one for the nose. With the now-sticky toothpick, pick up the black nonpareils and push them into the holes.

3. To make the flippers, cut two flat triangles off the long sides of the second marshmallow. Cut away at the flatter short edge to reveal stickiness. To make the body, cut away a scoop on the edge of a second marshmallow. Press on the head. (Cut away more of the body marshmallow, if needed, to adhere the head.)

4. Press the flipper pieces to the sides of the torso. (Dust the cut bottoms of the flippers with confectioners' sugar if their stickiness is a problem.)

5. Display the seal on an aluminum foil "lake" surrounded by sugar snow, if desired.

SNOWMAN

Even this snowman's hat is made of a (chocolate-covered) marshmallow!

SUPPLIES

½ cup chocolate chips

2 regular marshmallows

1 chocolate wafer cookie (I used Nabisco Famous Chocolate Wafers)

scissors

toothpick

2 black nonpareils

6 to 8 black sugar pearls

1 orange gumdrop

1 jumbo marshmallow

1 piece of rainbow-striped sour belt candy (I used AirHeads Xtremes Rainbow Berry Sour Belts)

1 white frosted cupcake (optional)

1. To make the hat, melt the chocolate chips in a double boiler. Drop one regular marshmallow into the melted chocolate and roll it around with a fork until it's coated. Lift the marshmallow out of the chocolate with the fork and let the excess drip back into the bowl or pot. Carefully center it, flat side down, on the chocolate wafer cookie. Refrigerate to harden.

2. To make the head, cut a very thin sliver off the flat bottom of the remaining regular marsh-mallow. That sticky bottom will be the bottom of the head. Use the toothpick to poke five holes, two for eyes and three or four for the mouth. With the now-sticky toothpick, pick up

the nonpareils for eyes and sugar pearls for the mouth, and push them into the holes.

3. Use the toothpick to dig a bigger hole for the nose. Cut an angled piece off the orange gumdrop for the carrot nose. Roll it between your fingers to make it pointy. Cut a sliver off the back of the nose so that it is sticky, and push it into the hole in the head.

4. To make the torso, poke three holes into the jumbo marshmallow for the buttons. Use the toothpick to pick up the sugar pearls and push them into each hole.

5. Press the head onto the body. Put a dab of melted chocolate on top of the head and attach the hat on top.

6. Cut a strip of the sour belt candy in half along the length and tie it around the snowman's neck, for a scarf.

7. Put the snowman on top of the frosted cupcake, if desired, and press in. Place another sugar pearl "button" onto the frosting, if desired.

MONOGRAMMED HOT CHOCOLATE

Shaped marshmallows are fun for topping hot chocolate, oven s'mores, and more. Graphic, less intricately shaped cookie cutters, like letters, stars, and hearts, work well for this project.

SUPPLIES
cookie cutters

flat marshmallows (such as Kraft Jet-Puffed StackerMallows)

mugs of hot chocolate

1. Press the cookie cutter through the marshmallow.

2. Gently push out the cut shape.

3. Float the marshmallows in the hot chocolate.

SNOWY TREE CUPCAKES

These trees can be made with all jumbo, medium, or mixed marshmallow sizes. Presents and ornaments are optional.

SUPPLIES
scissors

1 jumbo or 2 regular marshmallows, or 1 jumbo plus 1 regular marshmallow

one 2½"-long candy stick

toothpick

pink jumbo nonpareils (optional)

1 white frosted cupcake

confectioners' sugar (optional)

Starburst Fruit Chews (optional)

1. To make the tree bottom, if you are using a jumbo marshmallow, trim two sides of one marshmallow at an angle to taper it, as shown, and reserve the scraps. (If you are using a regular marshmallow, cut two triangular pieces off and stick the cut sticky sides together to make a cone, as in the polar bear head on page 74.) Trim the top off of the tree bottom to make it sticky.

2. To make the treetop, use the jumbo marshmallow scraps or cut two triangular pieces off the second marshmallow, and stick the cut sticky sides together to make a cone. Trim off the bottom to make it flat and sticky, and put the piece on top

of the cut top edge of the tree bottom.

3. Use closed scissors to poke a hole into the bottom of the tree, and poke the straight candy stick into the tree.

4. If you're adding ornaments, use the toothpick to poke holes evenly all over the tree. With the now-sticky toothpick, pick up the pink nonpareils and push them into the holes.

5. Dust the frosted cupcake with confectioner's sugar "snow," if desired, and poke the tree trunk through the frosting into the cupcake. Surround the tree with Starburst Fruit Chews "presents," if desired.

COOKIES ARE A GREAT blank canvas for crafting. I love baking, and nothing tops homemade cookies, but there are times when you want to get right to the crafting. When you're making edible cake toppers and the cake is the real star, or you need an impromptu playdate activity and want to decorate cookies, or you're making gingerbread-style cottages and want to move on to covering the cottage with candy—**all these are perfect times to reach for store-bought cookies.**

I have a special place in my heart for the classic grocery-store cookies of my childhood and their very basic shapes: round chocolate wafers, tea biscuits, vanilla wafers, and others. Smooth, round Nabisco's Famous Wafers of icebox cake fame are an essential base for several projects in this chapter. Graham crackers, which come in honey or chocolate, are the perfect building blocks for **cookie cottages.** Use the pretty scalloped edges of shortbread cookies and tea biscuits in projects like flowers or castle-cake doors.

Cereal is one of my favorite food groups, for eating as well as crafting. The **tiny *O*s, spheres, and squares** are begging to be used as beads, roof tiles and bricks, facial features, mini doughnuts, or whatever you or your child can dream up. The popular marshmallow-and-cereal mixture is perfect for creating solid shapes for everything from bricks and blocks to houses and mini "cakes."

OPEN-FACE FUNNY FACE COOKIE SANDWICHES

A fun after-school snack and activity in one, these goofy face cookie sandwiches get a little nutritional boost from **fruit, nuts, seeds,** and **peanut butter** "glue." **Chocolate hazelnut spread** and **chocolate chips** sweeten the treats. The blocky-headed people, animal, and made-up creature possibilities are endless.

Good supplies to have on hand are **almond slices, sunflower seeds, mini** and/or regular **chocolate chips, sliced raspberries** and **strawberries,** and **assorted round, square, and rectangular cookies,** such as **vanilla wafers, honey** and **chocolate graham crackers, chocolate wafers,** and **tea biscuits.**

COOKIE CASTLE CAKE

This cookie castle cake looks quite grand but couldn't be easier to put together. You can always make a smaller cake or a one-tier cake!

SUPPLIES

serrated knife

65 to 75 sugar wafer cookies

13 Vienna Fingers cookies

2 Nabisco Mini Golden Oreo Sandwich cookies

2 graham crackers

scissors

1 piece of colored origami paper (or any thin paper)

5 toothpicks

double-sided tape

5 sugar cones (the ones with pointy bottoms)

one 10" frosted layer cake (4" tall)

one 6" frosted layer cake (4" tall)

16 Nabisco Golden Oreos

2 cans store-bought vanilla frosting, or about 3 cups homemade buttercream

4 wafer cones (the ones with flat bottoms)

21 pieces of Kix cereal

2 extra-thin pretzel sticks

blue berries from Cap'n Crunch's Crunch Berries cereal (optional)

Note: Depending on the height of your cake and the brand of sugar wafer cookies you use, you may have to adjust the size of your "bricks" to get the alternating high and low segments of the walls. This cake's walls alternated with one full cookie and then a 1" cookie piece below a full cookie. The sizes and quantities listed above are what I used in the project shown but will be different if your cake is larger or smaller.

1. Use the serrated knife to saw the sugar wafer cookies to brick height (see note at left). For the bottom layer, I used thirty-four whole cookies and seventeen 1" pieces, and for the top layer, I used twenty whole cookies and ten 1" pieces.

2. Pull apart the Vienna Fingers sandwiches. Use the serrated knife to saw four cookie halves down to ¾" for the door tops and twenty-one down to 2" for the windows. Break one of the graham crackers in half to make the two sets of doors. (Shorten these dimensions for a smaller cake.)

3. Cut out five flag shapes from the colored paper and adhere them to the toothpicks with double-sided tape. Use the serrated knife to saw off the pointy bottoms of the sugar cones (just a tiny amount), and gently push the flag toothpicks into the small openings in the cones.

4. Put the 10" cake on a platter, and stack the 6" cake on top toward one side.

5. Lay the sugar wafer cookie bricks around the sides of the cakes in an alternating pattern, as shown.

6. Make two 8-cookie-high Oreo towers, using a small blob of frosting between each layer to "glue" them together, and place them in front of the smaller cake layer, as shown. Spread a little frosting on top of each tower top, and place a sugar cone with its flag on top.

7. Place two wafer cones toward the front of the very top of the cake. Put an inverted wafer cone centered behind them to form a triangle. Top each of the front two wafer cones with sugar cones and their flags. Put a blob of frosting on top of the inverted wafer cone and top with another wafer cone, as shown. Top that with a sugar cone and its flag. (Remove the cone and their flags whenever you have to move the cake, or add these at the last minute when the cake is in place.)

8. Use frosting to "glue" the windows, doors, and door tops. Lay the second graham cracker down, as shown, under the bottom layer's doors as a drawbridge. "Glue" the Kix cereal on as doorknobs and brick toppers, and the pretzel sticks on the draw-bridge as chains.

9. Spread blue cereal around the cake to create a moat, if desired.

CRISP RICE CEREAL TREAT LETTERS

An easy no-bake dessert, crisp rice cereal treats are more popular than ever because they are easily made gluten-free by using gluten-free crisp rice cereal and marshmallows. Once cool, they can be cut into many shapes.

To make a template, print out a large initial that will fit over the pan of treats, and cut out the letter. Make a double batch using the recipe on the side of the cereal box. Spread the mixture into a 9 × 13-inch baking dish. Let cool completely; once cooled, the mixture should not be sticky.

Turn the mixture out onto a cutting board, and flip it back over (so the sticky bottom is back on the bottom). Lay the letter template on top and use a serrated knife to cut out the shape.

You can cut the remaining scraps into any shape you choose. I made mini letter "petits fours." If fresh enough, the scraps can even be remolded to make a larger shape.

EASY COOKIE FLOWERS

Making flowers from store-bought cookies and candy is a simple and fun activity for younger kids and they look pretty on the side of a frosted cake. The **M&M** centers are "glued" to the cookie with a dot of **vanilla icing** that has been **tinted pink.** Pipe on the icing dots (see page 100 for how to make an easy piping bag).

Provide guests with **clean kid-safe scissors** and **green sour belt candy** to make stems and leaves, or precut the pieces for younger kids. The flowers pictured are made from **vanilla wafers** and **shortbread cookies.**

CEREAL HOUSES

These houses are made by molding cereal in empty milk cartons. Collect a variety of sizes to make a little village. One batch of crisp rice cereal should fill at least 2 pint containers or 1 pint plus two ½-pint cartons, and 1 batch of corn puff cereal should fill a ½-gallon carton (cut down to a height of about 7"), one ½-pint, and one 1-pint carton.

SUPPLIES
assorted empty containers (such as milk, cream, half and half, or orange juice cartons), washed and dried

scissors

masking tape

nonstick cooking spray

3 tablespoons butter

one 10-ounce bag mini or regular marshmallows

½ cup green berries from Cap'n Crunch's Crunch Berries cereal (optional)

6 cups crisp rice cereal (such as Rice Krispies) or 8 cups corn puff cereal (such as Kix)

pretzel sticks (optional)

gumdrops (optional)

toothpick (optional)

red berries from Cap'n Crunch's Crunch Berries cereal (optional)

1. Open the tops of the cartons and cut out the prefolded triangles on the two sides of the carton top, as shown. Close the carton back up and tape closed. Cut the bottoms off and cut the heights down, if desired. Spray the inside of the carton with nonstick cooking spray.

2. Melt the butter in large saucepan set over medium-low heat. Add the marshmallows and stir until melted. If you are making trees, put 1 tablespoon of the melted marshmallows into a bowl and stir in the green cereal. Stir in the crisp rice cereal.

3. Spoon the cereal mixture into a prepared carton, making sure to fill the pointy roof. Let cool.

4. To unmold the house, squeeze the sides of the carton to loosen, and then press on the top and push and shake it out. Repeat with the remaining cartons. Reheat the mixture on very low heat, if needed, to soften.

5. To make a tree, grease your hands with nonstick cooking spray and mold tree tops out of the green cereal mixture. Gently push a pretzel stick into the mixture as a trunk. To stand the trees up, cut a thin slice off the bottom of a gumdrop and place the sticky bottom onto the cake stand or serving plate. Use the toothpick to poke a hole in the top of the gumdrop and stick the pretzel stick inside.

6. Use leftover green cereal mixture to make "bushes" with red cereal "flowers," if desired.

COOKIE PLANETS

White chocolate is piped and brushed on cookies to create planet rings and stripes. These are a fun outer space party activity or treat.

SUPPLIES

one 4-ounce white chocolate bar

¼ teaspoon vegetable oil (optional)

sandwich-sized resealable plastic bag, for piping

rubber band or twist tie, for piping

scissors

assorted flat round cookies (such as Nabisco Famous Chocolate Wafers)

waxed paper

paintbrush and small bowl

assorted sanding sugars and/or nonpareils

1. Break the chocolate into somewhat even pieces and put in a stainless steel bowl. Place the bowl on top of a saucepan of simmering water (the bowl should not touch the water). When the chocolate is almost melted, turn off the heat and stir until the chocolate is fully melted. Add up to ¼ teaspoon vegetable oil, if needed, to thin the chocolate until it pours off a spoon.

2. To make a piping bag, put one corner of the resealable plastic bag in a small juice glass. Pull the rest of the bag over the sides of the glass. Fill the bag with about a cup of the melted chocolate. Twist the bag closed in your hands, tightly cinch it with the rubber band, and seal the bag closed. Cut the tiniest hole (less than ⅛") off the corner of the bag

with scissors. Squeeze out some chocolate to see if the hole is big enough. Enlarge the hole if needed by cutting off the tiniest bit of the bag until it pipes out a thick line of chocolate.

3. Line a baking sheet with wax paper and place the cookies on the sheet. Brush the remaining chocolate onto the cookies in wide transparent stripes. Pipe thin lines of chocolate next to or on top of the brushed lines.

4. Make rings by piping lines of chocolate across a cookie, extending ½" or less past the edges of the cookie.

5. Sprinkle the tops with the sanding sugar and/or nonpareils. Shake off any excess.

6. Refrigerate for at least 20 minutes to harden. Store in an airtight container, separated by layers of waxed paper, in the refrigerator.

COOKIE HOUSES

Gingerbread houses are fun to bake, build, and decorate, but these little houses allow you to skip quickly to the creative parts. While these are traditionally made for Christmas, try decorating them for other holidays or occasions.

BASIC HOUSE INSTRUCTIONS

SUPPLIES

4 graham crackers, honey or chocolate

serrated knife

Royal Icing (recipe follows)

piece of cardboard (at least 4" × 4"; optional)

small jar (like a spice jar)

assorted candies

1. To cut graham crackers, use a serrated knife and a very light sawing motion with almost no downward pressure. On one graham cracker, cut off some height (A), and then cut off the angles to form a peaked piece. Use the first peaked piece as a template for cutting a second peaked piece. Cut the remaining two graham crackers in half. Two will be used for the side walls and two for the roof.

2. Pipe a thin line of icing on the bottom of one side wall (make sure that the graham cracker perforations are going in the same direction on the side walls and roof pieces), and stick it onto the piece of cardboard (or a paper plate) off to one side. Use a small jar (like a spice bottle) to hold up this first wall (B). Glue one of the peaked pieces to the square wall piece by piping a thin line of icing along the bottom and the side edge of the peaked

piece. Attach the peaked piece just inside the back of the square wall. Repeat with the other peaked piece to attach to the other side of the square side wall. (Remove the jar when set.) Pipe a thin line of icing on the remaining side edges of both peaked pieces. Pipe a thin line of icing on the bottom of the last square wall. Attach the wall to the two peaked pieces.

3. Decorate the roof by piping a line of icing along the bottom of a cracker. Adhere a row of bottom "tiles" first, whether they are Necco Wafers or sticks of chewing gum on the Valentine's House (page 103) or sunflower seeds on the Halloween Haunted Cottage (page 102). Pipe another line above that row of tiles and let those candies overlap the first row (C). Repeat until the roof is covered. Repeat the process to make a second roof piece. Let dry for about 30 minutes.

4. Attach the roof by piping icing along the top edges of the wall and peaked pieces and setting the roof pieces on top (D). Cover the top seam by gluing on additional candy with Royal Icing, if desired.

5. With the icing, glue on the door, attic window, and other embellishments.

ROYAL ICING

SUPPLIES

electric mixer fitted with a paddle attachment (optional)

1 pound (1 box) confectioners' sugar

5 tablespoons meringue powder, plus more if needed

7 tablespoons water, plus more as needed

sandwich-sized resealable plastic bag, for piping

small juice glass

rubber band, for piping bag

scissors

1. In the bowl of an electric mixer fitted with the paddle attachment, or by hand, mix the sugar, meringue powder, and water until smooth.

2. If the icing is too thin, add meringue powder ½ teaspoon at a time until thickened. If it's too thick, add water. The consistency should be slightly looser than toothpaste.

3. To make a piping bag, put one corner of the resealable plastic bag in a small juice glass. Pull the rest of the bag over the sides of the glass. Fill the bag with about a cup of Royal Icing. Twist the bag closed in your hands, tightly cinch it with the rubber band, and seal the bag closed. Cut the tiniest hole (less than ⅛") off the corner of the bag with scissors. Squeeze out some icing to see if the hole is big enough.

A

B

C

D

HALLOWEEN HAUNTED COTTAGE

This spooky, spiky haunted cottage has its roof tiled with sunflower seeds still in their shells. Pipe some Royal Icing (page 100) at the roof seam, and add a row of upright sunflower seeds for a spiky top. The attic window is a larger white pumpkin seed also in its shell, the doorknob is a black sugar pearl, the window is a licorice allsort, and the black shrubs are black gumdrops and gummy raspberries. The ground is covered with Haribo Piratos black licorice discs, and the path is Necco Wafers. Approach with caution!

VALENTINE'S HOUSE

Bubble gum tape, sold by the roll and cut into strips, is the tiling for a sweet love shack (right). Display it on a tray covered with some shredded coconut as a Valentine's Day party centerpiece. The attic window (right) is a conversation heart and the top hook of a candy cane is the arched doorway. Another attic window (left) is a Kraft Jet-Puffed Heartmallow. Little Dum Dum lollipops poked into gumdrops are the trees. Nougat candies form a walkway (right).

COOKIE MONOGRAMS

The quickest and easiest of cupcake toppers, cookie monograms are wonderfully versatile. You make them by attaching **store-bought cookie letters** onto **store-bought wafer cookies** with **frosting "glue."** Other great "glue" options are **peanut butter** and **chocolate hazelnut spread.** To attach the letter to the cookie base, use the tip of a butter knife to put dots of frosting on the back of a letter, and then press it onto a wafer cookie. Try to keep the frosting in the center of the letter so that when you press it onto the cookie, the frosting doesn't squish out.

With these letters, you can spell the birthday boy's or girl's name, or personalize each guest's cupcake. I wedged them into the cupcake's frosting to stand them up, as shown, but they could also be placed flat on top.

SOURCES

True to the theme of this book, most items can be found at supermarkets or big box stores, with the exception of a few special supplies, like the large black nonpareils used for eyes. It's worth a little time to compile a toolkit of these special items, which can be found at party, baking supply, or craft stores.

CREATURE-MAKING AND CANDY BASICS BUILDING TOOLKIT

Nonpareils and sprinkles
Both are widely available but check these sources for special sizes, shapes, and colors (like large nonpareils, aka "sugar pearls" or "jumbo nonpareils").

Bake It Pretty (bakeitpretty.com)
Fancy Flours (fancyflours.com)
N.Y. Cake (nycake.com)
Party City (partycity.com)
Target (target.com)

Haribo Raspberries
I pluck the little sprinkles off these and use them as eyes.

The Candyland Store (thecandylandstore.com)

Black or red shoestring licorice *(common supermarket options are red Twizzlers Pull 'n' Peel or Haribo Black Licorice Wheels)*

Necco Wafers
Economy Candy (economycandy.com)

Sour belts *(red, blue, green, and striped)*
Nuts.com (nuts.com)

SPECIALTY ITEMS

Jolly Rancher Bold Fruit Smoothies
Amazon (amazon.com)

Black licorice starlight candies
Gilliam black licorice hard candy sticks
A Candy Store (acandystore.com)

Haribo Alphabet Letters
Amazon (amazon.com)

Trader Joe's Cinnamon Schoolbook Cookies
Trader Joe's (traderjoes.com)

Food coloring markers
Party City or Wilton Industries (wilton.com)

MATERIALS

Baker's twine, cellophane bags, striped straws, cupcake papers, and more!

Bake It Pretty (bakeitpretty.com)
Garnish (thinkgarnish.com)
Layer Cake Shop (layercakeshop.com)
Martha Stewart Crafts (marthastewartcrafts.com)
Michael's Stores (Michaels.com)
Shop Sweet Lulu (shopsweetlulu.com)

ACKNOWLEDGMENTS

THIS BOOK HAS BEEN A DREAM for so long and it would never have happened without an incredible team of supporters: Amy, my amazing photographer, collaborator, life coach, and dear friend; Carla Glasser, our wise and comforting agent; our editor, Ashley Phillips, for her passionate support; Robin Rosenthal for her amazing eye, design skills, and dedication to this project; Stephanie Huntwork for her thoughtful art direction; and Pam Krauss for her leadership and vision for this book. David Miao for all his technical photo expertise; Betty Wong, for believing in this book early on; Margaret McCartney for her generous and skillful crafting and emotional support; and Ellen Morrissey and Alex Postman for their sage advice when we were just getting started.

Martha Stewart, my mentor who inspires millions, and my whole extended MSLO family, including Gael Towey, Eric Pike, Deb Bishop, Hannah Milman, Megen Lee, Darcy Miller, Kevin Sharkey, Laura Normandin, Silke Stoddard, Marcie McGoldrick, and more names than I can fit here.

My parents, Adele and Sheldon Levine, who appreciated and encouraged every scribble from the start.

My family: my brother, David Levine, and sister-in-law Mary Oleszek; my mother-in-law RoseMary Muench and father-in-law Fred, whom we miss dearly; my sister and brother-in-laws Katharine and Greg Nemec and Allison and JP Williams. My nephews and nieces Jacob, Olivia, Piper, Margaret, and Alexander and almost-niece, Eve! My grandmother Gertie, Aunt Elaine and Uncle Stanley Kramer, Aunt Sadie, and Uncles Michael Levine and Rey Nacienceno. And Simone Gomes, who keeps my family sane.

Adam Forbes, we took over your house and I stole your wife—thank you for everything! Oliver, Owen, and Beatrice, thank you for craft help, modeling, and sharing your mom. Lauren and Ben Lowry and Lila and Noah, two of our favorite models. Lou and Jane Gropp, for raising Amy to try new things (and for a few editing suggestions along the way).

The many, many people who have surrounded me with creativity, inspiration, and love, including (alphabetically!) Melinda Beck, Annette Berry, Noel Claro, Tasha Claro, Sophie Glasser, Debra Goldman, Johanna Goodman, Jordin Isip, Anna Kola, Page Marchese Norman, Melissa McGill, Helen Quinn, Kait Rhoads, and Paul Slifer.

My boys, Sammy and Lionel, I learn something new from you every day. You make me so proud and happy!

And my husband, Fred, you make the day-to-day inspiring, funny, and fun. Thank you for seeing the potential in every day (and me!).

INDEX